THE POWER OF REPENTANCE

THE POWER OF REPENTANCE

First published in Malaysia by
Tertib Publishing
23-2 Jalan PJS 5/30
Petaling Jaya Commercial City (PJCC)
46150 Petaling Jaya, Selangor
Malaysia

Tel: +603 7772 3156

First Edition: January 2020

ISBN: 978-967-2420-01-9

Cover design: Miza Mumtaz
Transcription: Maryam Jameelah bt Azhari
Typesetting & Layout: Ainul Syuhada
Printed by: Firdaus Press Sdn. Bhd.

Contents

ACKNOWLEDGEMENT

As salamualaikum wbt wrt,

Verily all praise to Allah SWT. We praise Him and we seek his help and we seek forgiveness from the evil of our souls and the consequences of our actions. Indeed, whoever Allah SWT guides there is none that can misguide him and whoever He misguides, none can bring him back to the straight path.

I bear witness and I testified, there's not a deity that is worthy of our worship other than Allah SWT and I bear witness and I testified that Muhammad ibn Abdillah Al-Qurasy Al-Hasyimi Al-Arabi is his final messenger and his most perfect worshipper.

Chapter 1

THE SINNERS

My dear Brothers and Sisters in Islam, I want you to close your eyes for a second, remember and think about the latest sin that you have done. The latest act of disobedience. The latest act that made you feel guilty for doing that act. Ask yourself, how recent was this act? How long ago did I commit this act? And if all of us are truthful in this response, there is not a single person sitting here today expect that he or she will be able to think of something they have done today. In fact, in the last few hours.

Brothers and Sisters, the reality and the fact of that matter is that each and every one of us is a sinner. A disobedient sinner. We sin by disobeying Allah SWT constantly. We sin by day and we sin by night. We sin with our hands and we sin with our feet. We sin with our tongue and we sin with our eyes. In fact, hardly a portion of the day goes by except that we do something that we should not do or we fail to do something that we should have done.

So much so, that many of us fail to register the fact that we are committing a sin, and this is the worst. Sins become a part of our lives. It becomes a part of our habit. We do sins like we eat and drink. We do it as a part of our daily routine. Not even registering that a sin has been committed.

Some of the early scholars of Islam and the Sahaba, when they saw the status of the Tabiiun; The Tabiiun is the second generation of Islam. When one of the Sahaba, Anas ibn Malik, when he saw how the second generation has strayed from the first. He said, "I see you committing sins that you consider to be less weighty than the hair on your head. You consider it to be your hair. If we had done the same sin in the time of Prophet Muhammad SAW, we would have thought we were destroyed."

If this is Anas ibn Malik talking about the second generation of Islam, let me ask you what do you think Anas Ibn Malik would say if he was to see us here today? What do you think he would say that the majority of us did not even pray 5 times a day? When the majority of us have our money tainted with Haraam. When the majority of us are committing not just the minor but major sins on a routine basis.

What do you think he, or those in his time or even more so, what do you think the Prophet SAW would have said? Brothers and sisters, one of the companions lived a long age when he saw the status of society around him, he said "I don't recognize anything of what you do as being part of Islam except your prayers and even that, you are changing inside. I don't recognize your lifestyle, I don't recognize your characters, I don't recognize your emotions, I don't recognize what you are doing and what you are avoiding as being part of Islam except for the prayers.'

And that, even in our time, the prayer has been something that is almost abandoned by the majority of us.

Brothers and sisters, it is time that we think about how we live our lives, which we are doing in this life that Allah SWT has given us. One of the famous companions, Abdullah Ibn Mas'ud, he said the example of the believer with regards to his sins. Pay attention to this, it is beautiful. The example of the believer with regards to his sins is that he thinks he is a person sitting under a large mountain. The mountain is his sins, and he is scared that the mountain will collapse and destroy him.

The believer sees his sins like a mountain and that mountain will destroy him and this as opposed to the example of the munafiq, the hypocrite, and the evil person. The example of the evil person with his sins is that he sees his sins like flies that buzz around his face. All he has to do is move his hand and the flies will go away.

So, the munafiq trivialises the sins that he does and he considers them to be like the flies so he just needs to brush them away and they will fly away. Whereas the believer aggrandizes the sins. Sees the sins as much bigger than they are.

Now let me ask you a question; who does more sins? The pious believer or the hypocrite? There is no doubt that the hypocrite does more sins and that the believers do fewer sins and yet those believers take that small sins that he has and considers them a mountain and the hypocrite does huge sins, massive sins and he considers them to be trivial like flies.

The question is, and I ask myself this question and I ask you as well. How do I view my sins and how do you view your sins? Do you view them like flies that you just have to brush them away? Ignore them? When you think about them you change the topic? You just ignore it blank out? Or you view them like a mountain you have to account for?

This will give you the character and the category you fall into.

Oh Muslims, the Prophet SAW warned us even against the minor sins. He said the minor sins pile up like twigs, like small branches and indeed the pile of small branches can give a strong fire. What happens when you have hundreds of twigs, hundreds and thousands of small branches? It will become a huge amount that will give you a huge fire.

Each one of them you consider trivial but when you keep on adding it, what happens? That is why the Prophet SAW said anytime Allah SWT asked any person about this trivial sins, that city would be destroyed. Anytime Allah SWT asked you about this trivial sins, the sins you consider minor. You have no hope then because if you are to be accounted for all your trivial sins then you have no way to save yourself from the wrath of Allah SWT.

What then is the solution? What is the way out? There must be an exit. This exit, this solution has been very clearly emphasized in the Quran and in the Sunnah of the Prophet SAW. The Prophet SAW said every single son of Adam is a sinner. You cannot be a human being except if you commit sins. If not, you would be an angel.

If you did not commit sins, you will not be human anymore, you will be an angel. Angels do not commit sins. As for human beings, it is impossible for a human being to reach the level of perfection that he abandons sins. You are a human, and humans are bound to err. 'To err is human' is indeed true. It is exactly what the Prophet SAW said. Every single human being is a sinner.

But then what? If we are all sinners. Is that going to be it? All of us will be the same? The answer is no. The Prophet SAW emphasized "...and the best of sinners"

So there is a 'best'. A good category of sinners. Not all sinners are at the same level. The Prophet SAW said the 'best of them'. We are all going to sin but there is a 'best of them'

THE ACT OF REPENTANCE

The best of sinners are those who repent.

Repentance. Taubah. This is the solution. This is the exit. This is the means of cleansing sins that we have committed. There is no other solution, no other exit path except for this path of Taubah and that is why Taubah is not an option for us.

Taubah is not a voluntary act for us. Taubah is obligatory and not an optional. Taubah is mandatory upon each and every Muslims. Each and every human being.

Taubah is something we are required to do. It is not an option. When we know we are all sinners, when we know that every one of us is going to disobey Allah SWT. the only way out of this is to cleanse ourselves through the cleansing of repentance. That is why Allah SWT commands us to repent.

All of you should repent to Allah. This is addressed to me and you and to every Muslims.

"O you who believes. Repent to Allah with sincere repentance. Repent to Allah with full and true repentance" (*Al-Tahrim* verse 66).

In this verse, Allah SWT emphasizes that even repentance has many types. There is true repentance and there is sincere repentance, and Allah SWT asks us to always go to those types of repentance.

Brothers and Sisters, repentance is obligatory to all human beings. This means that even the Prophets of Allah SWT have to repent and that is exactly glorified, that the Prophets of Allah SWT, all of them, had to seek forgiveness from Allah SWT.

Our father, Adam AS, the first human being, he did something that Allah SWT told him not to do. He ate from the three that Allah said to not eat from it. Iblis disobeyed Allah when Allah commanded it. When Allah asked him to prostrate to Adam, Iblis said no. So both of them disobeyed. Adam and Iblis.

But let me ask you; are they the same?

Nauzubillah. Of course not. Why? Both of them disobeyed, but why are they not at the same level?

As for our father, Adam, he repented. Adam said "O Allah, I have committed a sin. If you don't forgive me, and if you don't have mercy on me. I would be of those who are destroyed." Iblis became arrogant and was rejected and became kafirin. Adam repented and so Allah accepted it from him and forgave him and he became a Prophet of Allah.

Iblis did not repent. Iblis was rejected and became arrogant and thus became the most accursed of Allah's creation.

Prophet Nuh AS also asked something from Allah SWT that he should not ask. He asked Allah to save his son and Allah had clearly told him do not ask for anyone who is not a Muslim to be saved and his son was not a Muslim. So when he asked Allah for something he should not have asked, Nuh AS repented.

"Oh Allah, If you don't forgive me, and if you don't have mercy on me. I would be of those who are destroyed". This is Prophet Nuh AS repenting to Allah.

Ibrahim and Ismail, when they were building the Kaabah, while they are building the holiest structure on earth, they made a dua to Allah SWT. "Forgive us and accept our repentance. Let us be those who repent and accepted. You are the one who accepts repentance."

Musa AS when he asked to see Allah SWT, and he shouldn't have asked this because he knows as all the Prophets do, that Allah cannot be seen. When he woke from the coma he fell into Musa AS said "Oh Allah, how insulted are you? I am guilty. I turn to you in repentance." Musa was not ashamed to repent to Allah.

And how about our beloved Prophet Muhammad SAW? Someone who Allah SWT has forgiven his every sin.

Allah says in the Quran "Every sins of yours We have forgiven it." The Prophet Muhammad SAW said, in a hadith of Sahih Bukhari, "Indeed I repent to Allah every single day more than 100 times." 100 times! I seek Allah's forgiveness every single day.

Let me ask you brothers and sisters, who are in need of Allah's mercy? Sinful people or the holiest man; Prophet Muhammad SAW?

The answer is obvious; we are more in need of Allah's mercy. So the question is; If the Prophet SAW would seek Allah's forgiveness 100 times a day, how often do you think we need to be seeking Allah's forgiveness?

REPENTANCE IS AN OBLIGATION

Oh Muslims, as we said Taubah is not an option, it is an obligation. Taubah is Farouq. It is obligatory for every single Muslim, every single day of his life. And anybody who reads the Quran and Sunnah cannot help but be overwhelmed by the mercy of Allah SWT and by the majesty of Allah SWT.

Allah SWT commands us to repent then he tells about how merciful he is. In one verse, Allah SWT tells us "Who can forgive your sins other than Allah SWT?"

In another verse, Allah SWT says "Allah is the one who accepts your repentance and forgives your sins." And yet another verse Allah SWT says, "O you who believes, O you who committed sins'" Allah is addressing the sinners. "O you who have committed sins against your own soul do not despair of the Mercy of Allah. Indeed, Allah can forgive all sins."

In fact, we all know that Allah SWT has many names. Of them are 99 that are extra special and most of these names centres around the concept of mercy and forgiveness. Ponders upon the name of Allah, Ar-Rahman Ar-Rahim. The one who has mercy and the most merciful. The one who forgives and the one who omit all the sins. The one who erases, the one who causes you to repent and then accepts that repentance.

So many of Allah's names and attributes centres around the concept of mercy. Allah SWT reminds us in the Quran and the Prophet reminds us in the Sunnah about how magnificent is the Mercy of Allah SWT.

The Prophet SAW said in one hadith "That Allah SWT stretches out his hand on the day to accept the one who sins at night and Allah SWT stretches out his hand at night to accept the one who sins during the day." (Sahīh Muslim 2759)

So great is the mercy of Allah that the Prophet SAW even said "If the non-Muslim only knew how much mercy Allah has, even he would not give up hope to enter Jannah. If the non-Muslim only knew and realized how much mercy Allah has, even he would be enthusiastic with optimism and said: "Perhaps, I could enter Jannah as well."

When Syaitan was expelled from Jannah, Syaitan challenged Allah and said "I swear by your honour" and Syaitan was swearing by Allah's honour. "And I swear by you, Ya Allah, I will misguide each and every one of them". (Al-Hijr verse 39)

"I will misguide each and every one of them. This is my duty now," this is what syaitan said. This is what I want to do. Each and every one I want to misguide." He was talking about all of us.

What did Allah SWT respond?

Allah said, "And I swear by my own Izzah, that I will continue to forgive them as long as they turn to me in repent. Do what you want I will continue to forgive as long as they turn to me and ask me for repentance."

Allah himself ask us to repent to him. "Why don't they repent to Allah? Why don't they seek Allah's forgiveness? For Allah is Ghafur and Rahim." Allah tells us in the Quran if you repent it is for your own good. "If you do taubah it is for your own good."

Allah wants to accept your repentance. Allah wants to do so. We only need to show our repentance and Allah SWT will accept it. And the Prophet Muhammad SAW also reminded us of how much Allah loves to forgive.

When Aisha RA asked Rasulullah SAW "What should I say in Lailatul Qadr? On the holiest night of the year, what should I say?" The Prophet SAW said you should say "O Allah you are the one who is a'fu, the one who loves to forgive therefore forgive my sins as well."

Brothers and Sisters, one of the biggest sins that we can do are to give up hope in Allah's forgiveness. To claim that Allah cannot forgive you is a bigger sin than any other sins you have done. Let me repeat that.

To claim that Allah cannot forgive me "I am too sinful. There is no point in repenting. Allah cannot forgive me because I am too sinful". This very claim of yours is the biggest sins than any you could have done as a Muslim. No question about it.

Why and how so?

O Muslim, no matter how sinful you are, do you think you alone, single-handedly have committed so many sins that you can encompass Allah's mercy? That Allah's mercy cannot forgive you and you can challenge the Ar-Rahman and the Rahim. That you can say "I am so sinful".

Who are you and what are your sins in comparison to Allah's Mercy? To be able to claim that you are sinful and Allah cannot forgive you.

Arrogance is the greater crime and the greater sin than any of the sins that you might have done and that is why the Prophet SAW mentioned the biggest sin is shirk. To worship another God, to worship an Idol. The biggest of all sins is shirk, to give up hope in Allah's mercy and to say that Allah cannot forgive me.

These are the biggest sin to commit. To claim that Allah cannot forgive you, you are limiting the mercy of Allah. You are limiting the forgiveness of Allah.

You are claiming single-handedly that you and your sins are more powerful than Allah and His Mercy.

Allah SWT challenges us in the Quran "Say O my servants who have committed sins against themselves, O you who have lived your life in evil, O you who have not prayed regularly, O you who involve in drugs and women and alcohol and the evils on earth. Do not give up hope for Allah's mercy". The verse in the Quran addresses the sinners, evil people, evil Muslims.

O you who are sinners, do not give up hope for Allah's mercy. Allah can forgive all sins, no exception. Even the sin of shirk, Allah forgives it when somebody repents. How do you repent from shirk? By restating your shahadah and never returning to that Syirk again.

Even the sin of shirk, Allah forgives it. When someone converts to Islam, Allah forgives his sins, is it not? If a Hindu, Christian or any person accepts Islam, the shirk he has done is all forgiven. Similarly, if a Muslim commits Syirk, he must say the shahadah again, and with that shahadah, repent, and even the sins shirk will be forgiven.

How about other sins that are lesser than that?

Brothers and Sisters, there is no question that Allah's forgiveness and Allah's mercy can encompass all of the creation. You all know of the famous hadith of the Prophet SAW where he said that the Prophet Musa AS was with the famous Khidir.

Khidir, by the way, was a Prophet of Allah. Some people think that he was a mystical saint. This is not true. Khidir was another Prophet. Musa was also a Prophet. And the two Prophets were sent to two different people.

It is not possible for the Wali of Allah to be higher than the Prophet of Allah. When Musa is coming to learn from Khidir, this means Khidir was already a Prophet and Khidir has knowledge that Musa does not have and that is why Khidir did what he did and that is another topic of itself.

When Musa was with Khidir and Khidir was riding that ship, the story was mentioned in the Quran. He dipped his finger into the ocean and pull it out and he asked Musa, "How much water do you think my finger decrease from the ocean?"

Musa said, "Nothing. None has your water decrease the ocean." Khidir than replied, "Such is the Mercy of Allah and the bounty of Allah SWT that all the creation of Allah cannot detract, cannot subtract cannot reduce the mercy and bounty of Allah SWT just like my finger cannot reduce the oceans water."

Such is the mercy of Allah that no person can despair from it.

Chapter 4

THE METHODOLOGY OF REPENTANCE

The question arises, "How do we go about this process of Taubah? What is the proper methodology of Taubah?"

The proper methodology of Taubah is very simple. There are a number of steps, memorized them. They are very simple.

The first step in our procedure of Taubah; We must repent for the sake of Allah. We don't repent because somebody saw us doing a bad action, we don't repent because we are caught redhanded. We repent for the sake of Allah SAW.

The second condition is that we must feel guilty in our hearts. Brothers and Sisters, feeling guilty is the sign of Iman. Feeling guilty is the sign you have some faith. If you did not have any faith, you wouldn't feel guilty. So when you feel guilty, at least thank Allah that you have that much Iman that you feel guilty. No doubt if you have higher Iman, you wouldn't even commit the sin in the first place. But to feel guilty is a necessary requirement of repentance.

The Prophet SAW said, "Feeling guilty is the essence of Taubah. Feeling guilty is the heart, the prox of repentance."

The third thing that we must do is to seek forgiveness with our tongues as we have with our hearts. Do this by saying, "Oh Allah, I have sinned. Forgive me. Astaughfirullah. Atubu illah Allah. Allahuma afuun tuhibu affauana."

There are so many dua and if you don't know Arabic, say it with your mother tongue. Allah knows all languages. Allah wants to see your spirit and your heart, not the verbal things that you utter.

If you don't know Arabic, say it in your mother tongue. "Oh Allah, I have sinned, forgive me. Oh Allah, you are forgiving, you are the merciful. If you don't forgive me. There is no other being that can forgive me.

So it must be followed by a verbal act of repentance.

The fourth point is that we need to make an intention to stop the sin. If you steal money from somebody and then you meet them the next day and said: "Oh, I've stolen your money." But in your heart, you want to steal more money on the same day.

What type of repentance is this? It is not full repentance. It is not emitted to guilt.

You must make an intention not to return to that sin and it is important the most that you make an intention to not return. If you do return to that sin, that does not disqualify your previous repentance because Allah judges by intention.

If you return to that sin again, you must repent again and your first repentance is still valid. If you return the third time, you repent the third time. If you return the fourth time, you repent the fourth time.

You sinned, again and again, you repent again and again. An infinite cycle until you meet your Lord on the day of judgement.

There is a tactic of Syaitan. A plot of Syaitan. For example, some of us are addicted to a sin whether it is taking drugs or smoking whatever the sin might be, we are addicted to it. So we repent one day and feel guilty.

We say "Oh Allah, that is it. That is the last drink I will ever have. Never again will I return to that sin. A day goes by, a week goes by, a month goes by, 3 months go by and then Syaitan comes and you slip and drink again.

You feel guilty and you repent again. You said that's it, that's the last time. Instead of 3 months, you slip in 2 months that you return to the alcohol again. This time instead of 2 months, you return to alcohol in 1 month.

Now syaitan come to you and said, "You know what? Forget it. You are not going to be a good Muslim, ever. You might as well drink and enjoy life and worry about the Hereafter later on. Don't worry about repentance now, you are always an evil person."

You see, the person was being righteous and good until this thought came to him. Had he died in any of those repeated states, Allah will accept his repentance. But if he were to die in this state, here is where he'll be a major sinner.

Let me ask you a question: When a child is learning how to walk, does the child count how often he falls? Does the child fall for the first time then he stands up for the second time and the third time and said "You know what? Forget it. I am never going to learn how to walk. I'll crawl as long as I live."

No. The child will continually try over and over again until the child finally perfected the art of walking. Even as an adult we would sometimes trip once in a while. What do we do after we've tripped 10, 20, 1000 times in our life? Do we then lie in the dust and said "Forget it. I am never going to walk again." Or do we stand up and brush the dirt and continue walking?

And if we trip again, what do we do? We stand up and continue walking.

Such as the way with repentance, such as the way of Taubah. Allah does not count the number of times you repent, Allah looks at the quality of your Taubah and not the quantity of your Taubah. Allah looks at your quality of guilt and repentance and not the quantity of time you have asked Him.

O Muslim never lose hope of Allah's forgiveness.

So those are the conditions of Taubah:

1. Sincerity

2. Feeling regret and remorse

3. Seeking Allah's forgiveness verbally

4. Making an intention never to return to that sin.

And there's a **5th condition** if it involves another human being. If you stole some money, if you backbite someone, if you slander the person, then along with this 4 conditions, you also have to seek forgiveness from that person because you have wronged him, and you have wronged yourself and Allah SWT.

So if you have stolen somebody's money, you must return that money to him. Or if you don't know who the money is from, if you embezzle a fund or something, you must get rid of that money and give it to the poor. Expecting no reward, it is not your money in the first place. But you need to make it right, turn your wrong to right and that fifth condition is only when you have committed sins with another person.

Chapter 5

THE BLESSINGS OF REPENTANCE

Once you perfected your Taubah, what happens?

Firstly, Allah SWT will erase that sin. He forgives and he will also erase the sins. You see, we forgive but we don't forget. If somebody wrongs you, even if you forgive him at the back of your mind you remember "he did this to me" "he did that to me" and you will always be extra cautious.

Allah SWT forgives and he also erases the sin. No sin is left after the repentance. The Prophet SAW said, "The one who repents from the sin it is as if he never committed the sin at all."

The second thing after you perfected you Taubah, this is amazing brothers and sisters, when you sin and repent, Allah will substitute your evil with a good deed. You get rewarded for committing a sin. You get rewarded for the sins you've done. Not because of the sin but because of the Taubah.

Allah says in the Quran: "Whoever repents and do good deeds, Allah will substitute and exchange for the evil he has done. Allah will give a good deed in its place. You will be rewarded for the sins you've done as long as you repent from it."

The third thing that Allah promises to the repentant, Allah promises him extra blessings in this world. Extra money, extra children and wealth and health. Allah promises those who repent, the good of this world along with the Hereafter.

You can read this in the story of Nuh AS. The Prophet Nuh AS told his people: "I told my people to seek Allah's forgiveness, Allah is the one who forgives. After you asked for Allah's forgiveness, what happens? Allah will send rain to you, beautiful rain and Allah will increase your money and increase your children and Allah will give you gardens and rivers under them. When you repent, Allah will give you blessings of this world."

The final blessings we will mention is that repentance is one of the reasons you enter Paradise. Allah SWT said in the Quran: "The only people that will enter Paradise are those who had done Taubah."

The Prophet SAW said, "If you were to stop committing sins, Allah SWT will get rid of you and bring forth people who commit sins."

Why? Does Allah love sinners? No. Allah does not love sinners.

What did the Prophet SAW say? "He will bring a group of people who commit sins so that they will ask Allah's forgiveness and so Allah can forgive them." Allah does not love sin but he loves to forgive. Allah does not love the sinner but he loves the repentant.

And to be a repenter you have to be a sinner where you reach the stage of repentance.

CONCLUSION

I conclude this with a hadith from Prophet SAW. The Prophet SAW said, "On the day of Judgement will draw close to the believer and cover him up in a private covering and nobody can be between them. And Allah will ask him "Do you not do this sin? And the believer said yes.

And ALLAH will continue to count the believer's sins until he thinks that he is doom. Then Allah SWT will tell him "Just as I hid this sin from other people in this world, today I will also hide it now from the eyes of all. Just like when you keep it private between you and me and ask me for forgiveness, so today, I will cover up all of your sins, erase them and you will not be called out for them."

And that person will enter the garden of paradise.

Allah will not count how many times you repent. How often you turn to him. In a hadith, Qudsi Allah SWT said: "When a sinner commits a sin and raises his hand to Allah "Forgive me", Allah said to the angel "Look, my servant has sinned, I have forgiven him." And if he commits sins again, Allah will say it again. Will he say the sinner is hopeless? No, he said to His angel, O my Angels, bear witness that you testify that I have forgiven this servant no matter what he does. Why? Because he recognizes that I am his Lord."

What does Allah want from us? To turn to Him for forgiveness. O Muslims, turn to the Ghaffar, Ghafoor, Rahim and if you do so, Allah will accept your repentance and bless you in this world and the Hereafter. That is the courageous man, that is a true sinner.

May Allah bless us to be among those who repent from their sin and accept that repentance and resurrect us in the Day of Judgement in the company of Prophet Muhammad SAW.

Q&A SESSION

QUESTION:

You said in the lecture that no sinner could challenge the Mercy of Allah. Does it mean that Iblis place in the Hellfire is guaranteed or does he has an opportunity to repent?

(Khasyiful Haq, ex-fashion designer)

ANSWER:

This question deals more with the topic: Qadr and it is a detailed topic to discuss. Suffice to state that in His infinite knowledge, Allah already knows that certain being's status such as Abu Lahab. When the Surah Al-Masad was sent down, Abu Lahab was still alive. It will be a big contradiction if he suddenly were to pronounce himself as a believer. So Allah knows the status of his faith and that he will never accept Islam. This is the same as Iblis. Allah knows the status of Iblis and tells us that he will be destined to go to the Hellfire. Along with Firaun and others like him. So theoretically, there is no being that is beyond Allah's forgiveness if that being repents. But realistically and practically, Allah has warned us of certain people who will never repent and one of them is Iblis.

QUESTION:

Part of repentance is seeking forgiveness from the person you wronged and if you slander or backbite them, do we need to tell why we ask them for forgiveness? Wouldn't that hurt the person? And in the Day of Judgement, Allah will cover us if we hide our sins so how is this possible when we open up our sins in order to ask for forgiveness?

(Sufi, student)

ANSWER:

Basically if you have done a sin against another person and you publicize it, it is more problematic. If you have slander someone than after you ask for Allah's forgiveness, you have to go to the people you slander to and admit the lies you spread about that person. Replace all the negative remarks with praises. If you meet the person you slander or backbite about, ask for forgiveness in a general manner like "Sorry for all the bad things I have done to you. I seek forgiveness." This is the way to get out of the sin.

QUESTION:

Is there any way by which we can recognize that Allah SWT accepts our repentance and good deeds?

(Muhammad Minatullah, Practicing doctor)

ANSWER:

The short answer is Yes and No. No, because no Muslim can ever guarantee that Allah has forgiven them. It is like saying "I am a person from Jannah" and no Muslim should say that. Instead, you should hope and expect Allah to forgive you. There is a difference. The sign for this is that you live a better life after your repentance than before. If you have been a sinner for years and when you repent, your future is brighter then that is the sign that Allah has accepted your repentance. If Allah tests you, this is a sign of Iman. Iman is proportional to the level of Iman you have.

QUESTION:

There is a fatwa from Sheikh Salim that it is not good to pledge to Allah SWT to never return to the sin because there is a possibility that we will return to that sin. How to repent after we return to the sin even after we have pledged to Allah SWT?

(Abdul Rahim, Chemical Engineer)

ANSWER:

There is a difference in making a promise or oath never to return and making an intention never to return. If you make an intention, this is what is required. If you make an oath, you have placed yourself in a predicament. What if you return back to the sin? So it is better to not bind yourself to it because you don't know if you will return to that sin or not. Rather, make a prayer to Allah "Oh Allah help me to not return to the sin again".

QUESTION:

As part of the methodology of Taubah, one is asked to make a prayer. Today, there are a lot of muftis who conduct Solat Taubah. Is there any authentic hadith that encourage this prayer?

ANSWER:

One of the signs of good repenter is increasing one's good deeds or when you repent it is encouraged that you do good deeds after like reading the Quran, Zikir and such. There is no clear indication of Solat Taubah but it is encouraged to increase one's prayers after they sin as this is stated in the Sunnah. Make it a habit to do good deeds after you sin and ask for forgiveness. Any good thing that you do is a sign of repentance and Allah knows best.

QUESTION:

Can we make repentance for others and what are the rewards for making repentance for others?

(Nasimah, homemaker)

ANSWER:

You cannot make repentance on a specific sin on behalf of others. You can only do it for yourself. What you can do is ask Allah to forgive that person and there is a difference between repentance and forgiveness. Repentance is "I have committed a sin, forgive me". Forgiveness is "Oh Allah, forgive my parents, grandparents, all Muslims". This is forgiveness. You make dua for other Muslims, no problem but repentance can only be done for yourself and your own sins. Taubah is individual. Unfortunately, there is a habit in some places that you do to a mediator for repentance. This is a catholic practice. It is not in Islam. Go directly to Allah and ask for forgiveness just like when you make sin to Allah. Though as a Muslim you can ask forgiveness for others.

QUESTION:

This is regarding addiction in doing sins. Sometimes we make sin and repent and when we do it again we tell ourselves not to worry because Allah is the most merciful and will forgive me. But we are asking for forgiveness, we are sincere and feel guilty. Is this type of repentance hypocrisy?

(Khasyiful Haq, ex-fashion designer)

ANSWER:

It depends on the mentality of the one who committed the sins. A true believer should always be conscious of Allah's attribute. When he sinned, in the back of his mind he feels guilty and asks Allah's for forgiveness. This is the sign of Iman. Rather than feeling confident that Allah will forgive. That arrogance is the sin here. It is not the affirmation of Allah's mercy that we need to question. So it goes back to your mentality. If your mentality is to submit and felt guilty, then this is the sign of Iman. But if your mentality is to be arrogant and confident, this is the sign of hypocrisy.

QUESTION:

For me, each Demi-God is the manifestation of the one true God. By worshipping the Demi-God, I am worshipping the ultimate God. How is this a sin?

(Rickum, Auditor-Non Muslim)

ANSWER:

This goes back to the very concept of God. what does it mean to be a God? By definition, God must be perfect all by himself. If there is more than one God, it'll be chaos in the work because each God wants all the power. The reason why the creation lives in harmony is that there is only one God. God cannot separate his attribute, all of the attributes have to be within him. That is how Islam differs than other religion. You said you worship this deity and that deity when in fact, it has to be one.

You cannot refer to God as a symbol or something you create. That is why in Islam, there's no image of God but instead, we are asked to bow down to Him. So your question comes back to the question, what does it mean to be a God?

QUESTION: [Follow Up Question]

We believe in Hindu philosophy where we concentrate on semi and demi-gods first and work our way to the ultimate God. So when we do, we are worshipping the ultimate God. It is just an analogy. Is that wrong too?

(Rickum, Auditor-Non Muslim)

ANSWER:

We cannot use an analogy to relate it with theology because everyone can give their own analogy. Our religion is not based on analogy. Our religion is based on what Allah tells us, it cannot be based upon a metaphorical conception. Your reason being you need a concentration, in this concentration, you have just created an entity. Whether you call it a God or a Demi-God. No entity deserves that kind of dedication. By your own testimony, you have admitted that this is a figment of your own imagination. It doesn't exist then why do you need it? Islam differs than other religion when we know that Allah is the only deity we don't need a fictitious middle man. We turn to Allah directly.

QUESTION:

If we hurt and wronged our non-Muslims friend, do we still need to ask for forgiveness?

ANSWER:

Brothers and Sisters, we are Muslims. We are not like any other religion who have double standards. To steal from a Muslim is a sin, to steal from a Hindu is a sin too. It doesn't matter what the ethnicity, gender or religion of the other person. The Law of Islam is applicable unto YOU. Doesn't mean if the person is of another religion you can abuse that. This is the beauty of Islam. It doesn't have double standards. What you have done to a Muslim, is the same if you have done to a non-Muslim. You still have to ask forgiveness from them in this world.

QUESTION:

You mention Allah's mercy is boundless but in there is a hadith that Allah says to the Prophet "Oh Prophet, there will be something that misguides you that says I am merciful". Isn't that contradictory?

(Aktar Habibi Shah, Lecturer)

ANSWER:

No, that is not an authentic hadith. I can guarantee you that much as it contradicts hundreds of verses in the Quran and the Prophet's Hadith. Allah proclaims that "I am the Merciful", "I am the forgiver", "I am the one who erases sins". But what is problematic is to feel confident that Allah will forgive you, and not affirming of Allah's Mercy.

QUESTION:

If I backbite a person and want to ask for forgiveness but before I manage to seek forgiveness, he dies. What should I do?

(Mansur Ahmad, Software Professional)

ANSWER:

What is important is your intention. If you are sincere in your repentance, and you don't have the chance to ask for forgiveness then go to the people you backbite or slander to and praise him just like to backbite him. Clean your tongue by spreading kind words to replace the bad words you said about him. That is the requirement of the Taubah if you want to repent.

QUESTION:

According to the Hadith mentioned that Allah will conceal our sins in the Day of Judgement as we had but what about the previous sins that we committed and out of ignorance expose it to others. Will Allah still conceal it or disclose to others?

(Afri, Student)

ANSWER:

No matter what you have done in the past, there is always a hope of Mercy. Worry about the present and the future. What happened has happened. The Prophet SAW said "Allah will forgive everyone, except those who openly talk about their sins. The Sahabah asked, "Who?" "Those who sin at night and in the morning tells people what he did" In other words, boast and brag about their sins. You have to be ashamed of the sins you made. You can disclose your sins if as a means to advise people so they can learn from it. What is prohibited is if you are proud of your sins. Rasulullah SAW said Allah will never forgive those who are like that.

Notes

Notes

Notes